ITCHY FEELINGS

by

Sherry Hall

Sherry Hall

Itchy Feelings

ISBN-13:978-1724358745
ISBN-10:172435874X

Sherry Hall

Itchy
Feelings

Sherry Hall

Have you ever gotten a wool sweater that was a gift from a special relative? Thanks...but when your Mom makes you wear it, it's so itchy and irritating it's all you can think about. You push the sleeves up, you pull them back down, you pull it away from your neck, then you scratch your back against the wall. You don't know what to do with yourself. You're getting hot, so you blow on your skin like a fan. Your Mom says, "Stop fidgeting! Think about something else. Stop scratching! Show more self control."

So you tap your foot, you hold your breath, you say the alphabet backwards, you think of all the colors you can and say them in Pig Latin. Nothing seems to help you pretend that you don't have an itch. You DO have an itch, lots of them. You don't know what else to do so you lose your self control and ATCH-SCRAY!

SCRATCH! SCRATCH! SCRATCH! SCRATCH! ....Ahhhhhhh.

But the better feeling only lasts a minute and the itching starts up again.

You are still miserable because you didn't solve the real problem that caused the itching. What would fix what's really wrong? Light bulb moment! You run upstairs two steps at a time and find your favorite blue comfy cotton t-shirt in your dresser and put it on your irritated skin where the itchy sweater used to be. Whew....you let out a big sigh as your skin takes in the cool softness. (Then you wad your itchy sweater into a ball and hide it way under your bed with the dust bunnies!)

I saw what you put under there.

Sherry Hall

Or how about this? Did a mosquito ever bite you? Or have you had an itchy rash? All you can think about is I HAVE TO SCRATCH! It does no good to wish it away or to hear your Dad say, "Don't scratch! You'll get an infection!" Your fingers are like a magnet to wherever the itch is, even when you sit on your hands to try to forget.

There's no real relief until you solve your problem. The blue t-shirt won't solve it this time but when your Mom puts some special cool cream made just for times like these on the red, itchy spot, it puts the fire and the itchiness out.

Feelings are a lot like that. If you don't know how to deal with the real problem behind your feelings, they can turn itchy. It can become all you can think about and the itchy feelings come out one way or another. Itchy feelings can be loud and messy, sometimes with attitude and a bad mood, and sometimes with tears and tantrums. When feelings are itchy, they have taken over. You lose control and that's not a good thing. Feelings have become in charge of you, instead of you being in charge of your feelings. Itchy exploding words can be said that hurt other people's feelings (and their ears), or cause you to do something that others will think is just plain mean. It's sure

not the way to add to your friend collection.

Just as the answer to an itchy sweater is a soft cotton t-shirt and the

answer to an itchy mosquito bite is some cool anti-itch lotion your

Mom puts on just the right spot, the answer to itchy feelings is learning

what to do with feelings *before* they become itchy. There's no need to

spread your itchy feelings to everybody else. That only shows that

either you don't know what to do with your feelings, or you didn't stop

to do something about them before they had a chance to get itchy.

Like unwanted germs, itchy feelings can be contagious, too, but you

can be a superhero and stop an epidemic from happening.

When your feelings are about to get itchy, before you let that

happen, STOP! We know itchy doesn't feel good. Take a slow, deep,

breath. It will only take a few seconds. Take another one if you'd like.

After you take a breath, ask yourself what you are thinking about

whatever just happened. Are you thinking something was unfair, or

someone was mean, or that someone doesn't like you? Don't get mad at me but maybe, just maybe, how you're thinking about whatever just

happened is wrong. This is important because you are at an

intersection just like a car at a stop sign that has choices of which way

to go next. Your thoughts cause your feelings, your feelings cause

your moods, and your moods cause your behavior choices. You need

to be sure your thinking is right or the rest of it will be all wrong.

Be a detective and ask yourself what the other person's point of view is about what just happened. Put yourself in their shoes (not really because that could be stinky so just pretend). Replay the situation. What is the other person thinking about what just happened? If you were standing in their shoes, what would you see? What would you think? How would you feel? We call this their point of view. You have a point of view, and so does everyone else. Just remember when you don't agree with a friend, maybe they don't agree with YOU! They have their own point of view. Think about what happened right before. Could you have done or said something differently that would have made things turn out better?

The next important step is to see if whatever you are thinking about the situation is caused by a fact or an opinion. Facts sound like this. "The moon is lots of miles away." An opinion sounds like this. "We need to call the police! The moon is missing! It wasn't in the sky tonight. Somebody stole it." Or... "Tommy hit me in my stomach with the ball" (fact) versus "Tommy was mad and hit me with the ball

Sherry Hall

in my stomach on purpose" (opinion).   Neither is going to make your stomach feel better but when you find out that someone bumped into Tommy's arm as he was getting ready to throw the ball and that caused his aim to be all wrong, you find out that hitting you in the stomach was an accident.   Don't you make mistakes, too?   When you realize the facts behind the event, it should let some of the air out of your angry tire.   Deep breath now, please.

Let's recap. To keep your feelings from getting itchy, stop and breathe, figure out if your thinking is based on fact or opinion, and do your detective work to think what someone else's point of view might be about what just happened. Let's say you do all of the steps and it turns out that someone won the race fair and square and you're feeling jealous, or someone was unkind on purpose and you're feeling hurt, or someone cheated at a game and you're feeling angry, or someone is trying to leave you out because they don't want their other friend to like you better and you're feeling disappointed. Those aren't feelings you want to feel and they could become itchy in a hurry but before you let that happen, think about the big picture and what you already know about dealing with feelings. Or if you don't know, this book will give you lots of ideas.

Let's take a timeout for just a second or two. Have you ever thought about what kind of person you want to be? You do have choices. What do you want others to think about you? When others say your name, what words do you want them to think about next?

Sherry Hall

Do you want to be thought of as someone who loses their temper a lot or someone who pays people back in a mean way because they think someone did them wrong? Do you want others to think of you as a person who says bad words or who throws tantrums like your 3 year old sister? Or do you want others to think of words like kind, mature, friendly, or problem solver when they think of you? It's up to you and the choices you make. Sometimes you have to rise above the situation, protect your idea of who you really want to be and how you want to come across to others, and don't let someone else push your buttons. Be sure you are reacting in a way that you would be proud to hear about when someone tells your story. Don't let itchy feelings take over and hide the person you can be.

I guess I've got some thinking to do.

Sherry Hall

Sometimes people do things that we think are unfair, they hurt our feelings, they may misunderstand us, or they truly have been unkind. You are not responsible for other people's choices. It's not your job to teach them a lesson and don't give your energy away by keeping score and paying them back. Don't let them take up space in your head with you reliving what they said, or by replaying what happened again and again. Move on and put it in your imaginary "file" of rotten things that happened. Don't get stuck like a hamster on a treadmill. It won't get you anywhere to waste your time thinking about it over and over and over again. Focus on right here, right now. Don't let thinking about the person or the situation take away any of your precious moments when you could be having fun! Don't hold a grudge against somebody. Grudge rhymes with sludge. It's not a pretty word and grudges don't help. When we hold a grudge against someone, our lips may be pursed like a duck face selfie, our foreheads get wrinkled up, and our eyes are narrow slits. You may be trying to make a point but if you walk around like that, you may have trouble seeing where you are going.

I hope you're looking at me because I want you to see I'm still mad about something you did in Kindergarten.

Grudges not only make us look ugly but they use up energy that could be spent in a positive way. And do you honestly want your face to look like that?

If someone was unkind and thoughtless, use that information to make a better choice to avoid playing with them next time. They showed you that they weren't treating you the way they would like to be treated. It's their loss. You have choices. Find someone else to play with who appreciates you, or you always have yourself to play with. Enjoy your own company. What do you like to do when you are alone? Being alone doesn't have to mean that you're bored, and it's not the same as being lonely. Or you can tell them how you feel like this: "When_____________________________happened, it made me feel ____________________. Please don't do it again."

Use your words but be polite. Here are some other possible solutions. The same idea doesn't fit every time so having more than one possible way of dealing with feelings is helpful. Choose to be a peacemaker. Remember it's not always your turn to have it your way. Ask yourself if this is really that big of a deal. Would someone you admire get so upset over this or would he or she stay calm and problem solve? It's not being a chicken to walk away. Let it go and move on. Or sometimes situations call for you to say you're sorry. I'm sorry can mean lots of things like I'm sorry we're not getting along right now, or I'm sorry that we're missing out on playing together, or I'm sorry I don't feel like being with you right now. Or maybe you need to admit that you made a mistake. It won't hurt when you say it.

Have you ever tried to flip your thinking? Let's say your lunchbox was packed with your all-time favorites. What would be in your lunchbox? You had been counting down all morning until it was time to eat. Now the moment has come to go to the school cafeteria, your mouth is watering just thinking how good it's all going to taste, and all of a sudden, "Oh no!" You remember you ran out the door this morning because you almost missed the bus and because you were hurrying, you left your lunchbox on the kitchen counter. What a letdown and sure you feel sad and disappointed. Who wouldn't? Someone with itchy feelings may get angry and loud about it and take it out on everyone around them causing lots of indigestion.   The time to problem solve is before your feelings get itchy so here we go.

How can you solve this problem? You could starve until the end of the day to get attention. Bad idea. Or you could take someone else's lunch when they aren't looking. Really bad idea. Or you could flip your thoughts. Instead of thinking it's a bad thing, think about how this could be a good thing. Take a slow, deep breath. Think it through. Just like a coach, be encouraging to yourself. Start with what the problem is. You can't have your favorite lunch today. Now think of the opportunities this presents. Maybe there's something in the cafeteria you could try. You might even find out you like the way it tastes. Or you could calmly tell your teacher what happened and maybe she has an idea you haven't thought about yet. If she feels sorry enough for you, maybe you'll end up with something from the junk food machine in the teacher's lounge. Yum! Or you could play a little game with yourself and pretend you're eating your favorite chips when you're really taking a bite of the cafeteria's mashed potatoes. Make a joke out of it with the person sitting next to you. "Man, this tastes so good! Crunch, crunch, crunch." (Hopefully the school's mashed potatoes aren't really crunchy and you are just imagining munching on a salty chip or pretzel.)

Lunch may not turn out the way you wanted it to but you'll get through it. It's one lunch out of your whole life. If you live to be 100, that would mean you have 36,499 other chances at eating lunches that you enjoy. Tomorrow is another day to pack your all-time favorites. When you flip your thinking, you can say, "I've got this." Use your imagination and think about all the ways something you don't like could be a good thing. You can choose to be miserable, or flip your thinking. It's really up to you.

This is a good spot to stop and review one more time how you can prevent feelings from getting itchy.

*Something has just happened that is causing you to feel a certain way. What happened? What are you feeling?

*Stop and take a slow, deep breath so you can think clearly. Take deep breaths until you feel calm.

*Is what you are thinking about what just happened, based on facts or an opinion?

*What is someone else's point of view?

*What actions and words will you choose next that line up with the kind of person you want to be?

*Think of ways you could deal with the problem *behind* your feelings. Add to your collection of ideas and pretend to fill an imaginary toolbox over time that is ready for you with possible solutions.

Sherry Hall

If you need help figuring out any of these steps, talk it over with a trusted grownup.

We're almost to the end but before you the close the book, let's practice some of the strategies that you learned in this story.

Deep Breathing

You can practice deep breathing by sitting up tall and placing your hand on your upper stomach where your diaphragm is. This is where you want your deep breath to come from. Inhale deeply, hold it for a count of 4, and blow the air out of your mouth for a count of 4. Repeat. You can have fun practicing the blowing out part by using a pinwheel or bubbles. The more you practice this, the easier it will become for this kind of breathing to happen when you need it.

When you stop and breathe, you are helping your brain calm down and do its best thinking. When you are upset, your brain may be too revved up to make the choices you want to be proud about. Practice deep breathing ahead of time so you get good at it. Breathing is a quiet kind of activity so you can practice it anytime and anywhere. No one will even know, unless you pull out your pinwheel or bottle of bubbles!

Fact or Opinion?

Decide whether these statements are facts or opinions.

1. She wouldn't play with me at recess so she doesn't want me to be her friend anymore.

2. Everybody thinks my haircut looks ugly.

3. My book was on my desk and now it isn't.

4. I had money in my room and now I don't. My sister must have stolen it.

5. The bus driver made a seating chart so we know where to sit.

6. As I was getting off the bus, I told the bus driver that someone hit me but he didn't do anything about it.

7. Everybody should love tacos.

8. PE is my favorite subject.

9. I am the best soccer player in the world.

10. I was the fastest runner in a race.

Can you make up some of your own examples?

Sherry Hall

Thinking Chains

Look at the examples and then see if you can make your own chain of think→feel→mood→behavior.

This is what I **think**→ This is what I **feel**→ My feelings create this **mood**→ This mood is shown by my **body language, my words, and my actions.**

Everybody thinks my haircut looks ugly→That makes me feel sad and embarrassed→ I am in a grouchy mood→ I'll scowl at everybody and tell them to leave me alone!

I think I look cool with my new haircut→ I feel proud and feel that I look good→ I am in a friendly mood→ I have a smile on my face. I'm asking others to play.

Your turn:

Who Do I Want to Be?

I, ____,
(your name)

want to be a person who is known for ______________________________

____. I can

make this happen by ____

____.

When others hear my name, this is what I want them to think of me:

____

____.

The words I use sound like this:

____.

My behavior choices look like this:

____.

Three words that describe my best self are ______________________,

______________________and ______________________.

I am the one who can make this happen. I am in charge of the person I
choose to be. I need to be sure that my behavior choices and words
line up with the kind of person I want to be.